THE RACE TO THE
SOUTH POLE

By
Jim Pipe

School Specialty
Publishing

Columbus, Ohio

THE CAST

Robert Scott *1868–1912. Robert Falcon Scott was a Royal Naval officer and Antarctic explorer. He led a failed expedition to the South Pole in the ship* Discovery. *In June 1910, he set off again, this time on the ship* Terra Nova. *Tragically, Scott's entire eam died in March 1912 while returning from the Pole in terrible weather conditions. Scott's tale of bravery and endurance made him an English hero.*

Roald Amundsen *1872–1928. Roald Engelbregt Gravning Amundsen was a Norwegian polar explorer. He first made the headlines when he crossed the Northwest Passage linking the Atlantic and Pacific Oceans. Amundsen then planned to reach the North Pole, but after Robert Peary's team got there first, he set out for Antarctica instead. His team beat Scott to the South Pole. Amundsen led further expeditions in ships and planes.*

Ernest Shackleton *1874–1922. Ernest Shackleton took part in Scott's* Discovery *expedition. In 1907–1909, he organized and led the second British Antarctic expedition. In his 1914 expedition to cross the Antarctic, his ship* Endurance *was crushed in the ice. He sailed in a small boat for help in a remarkable journey across the south Atlantic ocean. In January 1922, he died while attempting to sail around the Antarctic.*

Fridtjof Nansen *1861–1930. Fridtjof Nansen was a famous Norwegian explorer, scientist, and diplomat. He first became famous during an expedition in 1888 while crossing Greenland on skis. In 1893, he sailed to the Arctic in the* Fram, *a ship later used by Amundsen. This journey took three years and was the first voyage to cross the Arctic Ocean. Nansen also did groundbreaking scientific studies on the nervous system and ocean currents. In 1922, he was awarded a Nobel Peace Prize for his work in organizing war prisoners and refugees after World War I.*

Lawrence Oates *1880–1912. Oates fought as a cavalry officer during the Second Boer War in South Africa. In 1910, Oates joined Scott's expedition to the South Pole, partly due to his knowledge of horses. Oates was a member of the team to travel the final leg to the pole.*

Olav Bjaaland *1873–1961. Bjaaland was a Norwegian ski champion and a key member of Amundsen's team that reached the South Pole. Bjaaland was also a skilled carpenter who modified the sledges on the trip so that they were much lighter.*

School Specialty. **Publishing**

Copyright © ticktock Entertainment Ltd. 2006 First published in Great Britain in 2006 by ticktock Media Ltd., Unit 2, Orchard Business Centre, North Farm Road, Tunbridge Wells, Kent, TN2 3XF. This edition published in 2006 by School Specialty Publishing, a member of the School Specialty Family. Send all inquiries to School Specialty Publishing, 8720 Orion Place, Columbus, OH 43240.

Hardback ISBN 0-7696-4722-7 Paperback ISBN 0-7696-4702-2
1 2 3 4 5 6 7 8 9 10 TTM 10 09 08 07 06
Printed in China.

CONTENTS

TO THE ENDS OF THE EARTH

In 1911, blinded by blizzards, two groups of explorers struggled over a harsh, icy landscape. One group was led by Norwegian explorer Roald Amundsen. The other group was led by British captain Robert Falcon Scott.

Come on, men. We must keep going!

Scott's team faced particularly harsh weather conditions.

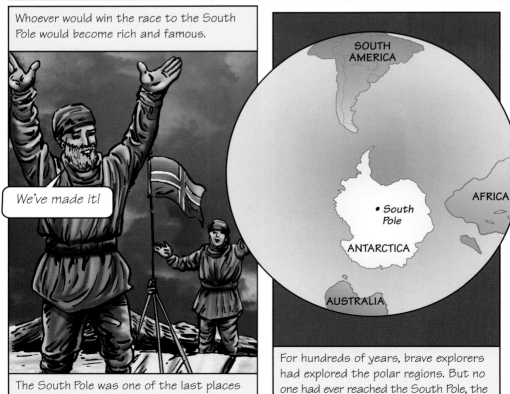

Whoever would win the race to the South Pole would become rich and famous.

We've made it!

The South Pole was one of the last places on Earth to be explored by human beings.

SOUTH AMERICA

AFRICA

• South Pole

ANTARCTICA

AUSTRALIA

For hundreds of years, brave explorers had explored the polar regions. But no one had ever reached the South Pole, the most southern point on Earth.

The sea voyage to Antarctica took several weeks. Once there, it was a 1,491 mile trek across icy mountains to the South Pole. In winter, the temperature would drop to -119°F.

In 330 B.C., the Greek explorer Pytheas crossed the Arctic circle and reached the Arctic pack ice. His crew were the first people to see the midnight sun.

The sun never sets in this strange land!

A thousand years later, Vikings sailed in Arctic waters. These fierce warriors from Norway and Denmark sailed across the Atlantic in their longships.

Look for seals. We are running short of food!

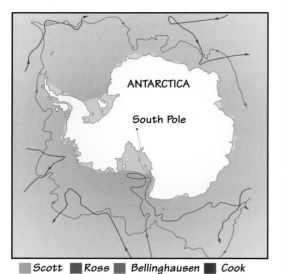

ANTARCTICA

South Pole

Scott ■ Ross ■ Bellinghausen ■ Cook

Many explorers have tried to reach the South Pole, here are some of their routes.

In January 1773, Captain James Cook and his English crew sailed around Antarctica without ever seeing it.

Iceberg on the starboard bow.

In 1739, Captain Jean-Baptiste Bouvet tried to claim the undiscovered "South Land" for France. He reached Bouvet Island, 994 miles north of Antarctica.

These birds have flippers, not wings!

Cook came within a day's sail of the coastline, but heavy pack ice forced him to turn back.

I'm sure it's out there...

In 1820, Thaddeus von Bellinghausen of Russia led the first expedition to see the Antarctic coastline, beating an English ship by only a few days.

Look at the size of this great new world!

In 1827, Captain William Edward Parry led a failed English expedition to the North Pole.

In 1841, James Clark Ross found a route through the ice pack to the coast of Antarctica.

He also discovered the Ross Ice Shelf and the smoking volcano of Mount Erebus.

In 1842, John Franklin led an expedition to find a route through the ice from the Atlantic to the Pacific.

Franklin and 128 of his men died from cold, disease, and lack of food. However, Franklin became a hero and the inspiration for two young boys named Robert Scott and Roald Amundsen.

FAST FACT Local Inuit people knew how to survive in the icy environment that killed Franklin. Later Polar explorers used Inuit methods, such as wearing snowshoes.

YOUNG EXPLORERS

Roald Amundsen was born on July 16, 1872, into a family of tough sailors and shipbuilders from the stormy Hvaler islands in Norway.

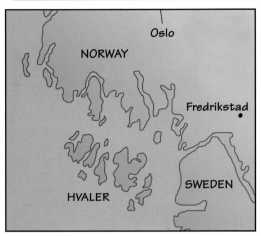

Roald Amundsen was born on 16th July, 1872, into a family of sailors and shipbuilders from the islands of Hvaler, in Norway.

Roald grew up in Christiania (now Oslo). As a boy, he loved playing outdoors. Skiing was very popular in Norway, and Roald learned to ski as soon as he could walk.

Hurry up, Eric! I'm in training.

Wait for me! You're too fast!

Eric, a shipbuilder who worked for Roald's father, taught Roald and his brothers about boats and sailing.

Why are you so interested in boats, Roald?

One day, I'm going to be an explorer!

Roald always slept with the windows open, even during the freezing Norwegian winters.

Leaving the window open will make me tough!

Roald's mother wanted him to be a doctor, but Roald wanted to be like Fridtjof Nansen, the famous Norwegian explorer.

Roald Amundsen grew into a tall, strong man with fair hair and deep blue eyes. He was determined to be in excellent physical shape.

You're the last of the Vikings, Roald!

73...74...75... Gasp!

In 1893, Amundsen saw Nansen's new ship, the *Fram*, set sail from Christiania. He was determined to go on his own polar expedition.

One day, I will set sail for the poles!

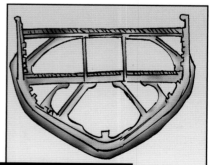

FAST FACT The *Fram* had a revolutionary design. The ship was shaped like a dish, so that it would be lifted above the floating ice rather than crushed by it.

As part of his polar training, Amundsen made long cross-country skiing trips in the mountains with his friend, Laurentius Urdahl.

I'm exhausted. Let's camp near here.

Come on. Let's do a few more miles.

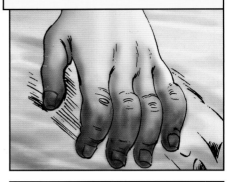

In 1896, Amundsen joined his first Antarctic expedition.

Welcome aboard the Belgica, Mr. Amundsen.

Amundsen fell in love with the icy landscape. He also learned a great deal from experienced explorers on the expedition.

It's so quiet and beautiful out here.

It's deadly, too. You never know when a blizzard will hit.

In 1903, Amundsen first made the headlines when he led a 65-foot fishing boat through the Northwest Passage, the same journey that had killed his hero, John Franklin.

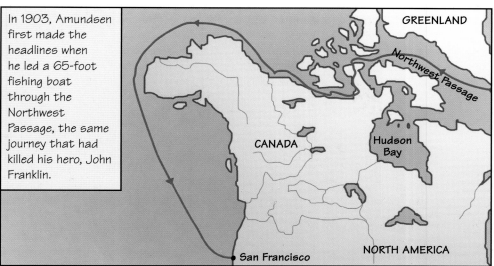

The journey to and from Antarctica took three years. During the winters, the ship was trapped in the ice.

We can't go any further. The ice is too thick.

Amundsen tried to reach the magnetic North Pole on foot, but failed.

Inuit hunters showed Amundsen how to dress warmly in loose furs, how to drive dog sleds, and other survival skills.

These dogs will keep running for hours!

Back home, in Norway, Amundsen became a hero.

Robert Falcon Scott was born on June 6, 1868. He grew up near the naval dockyards in Plymouth, England.

Scott was a sickly child who did not go to school until he was eight.

You need to rest, Robert.

At 13, Scott was sent into the navy by his father. Two years later, he joined his first ship. It was a tough, brutal life. Even in rough seas, young officers worked in the rigging 130 ft. above deck.

Hurry up, Scott. The storm is getting stronger.

For 10 years, Scott was a junior officer sailing all over the world. Then, in 1894, Scott's father became bankrupt. He died four years later, as did Scott's brother.

My family depends on me. I need a promotion to make more money.

Then, by chance, Scott met Sir Clements Markham, who was organizing a British Antarctic expedition.

Britain needs to get there first!

Sir Markham, I'm the man for the job.

Scott saw his opportunity. He persuaded Markham to make him leader of the expedition, even though he had no polar experience.

I know you won't let me down.

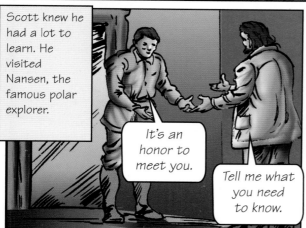

Scott knew he had a lot to learn. He visited Nansen, the famous polar explorer.

It's an honor to meet you.

Tell me what you need to know.

On Nansen's advice, Scott bought 23 dogs in Russia.

Dogs are the quickest way to travel over ice.

Over the next year, Scott made detailed plans and picked his crew. This included Ernest Shackleton, who later became a famous polar explorer. Meanwhile, a new ship, HMS Discovery, was being built for the expedition.

FAST FACT Scott and Shackleton went up in a hot air balloon on February 4, 1902, to get a view of the expedition area. The balloon sprung a leak and wasn't used again.

Scott's first British Antarctic expedition left England in July 1901. It reached Antarctica in early 1902, sailing along the coast past the area explored by Ross.

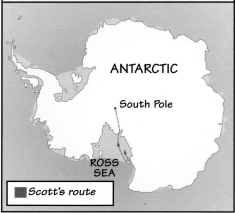

ANTARCTIC

South Pole

ROSS SEA

■ Scott's route

A hut was built for on Ross Island for storage and work space.

I'll get the dogs ready.

We should do some practice sledge runs.

In December 1902, Scott headed for the South Pole with Shackleton and Wilson. In 93 days they traveled over 932 miles, but bad weather, hunger, frostbite, and exhaustion forced them to turn back. The following year, Scott explored Victoria Land with Lashly and Petty Officer Edgar Evans. Blizzards again forced them to head for home.

The dogs are suffering badly.

This blizzard is going to bury us alive!

On their way back, Scott and Evans fell into a deep crevasse.

Aaaaaahhhhhh!

Scott and Evans were left dangling above a dark chasm with sheer walls of ice on either side of them.

Hang on!

Amazingly, Scott swung his feet around and gripped the wall with his crampons. Using the last of his strength, Scott climbed out safely.

I'm trying!

Then, Lashly pulled Evans up.

Keep pulling!

Back in England, Scott was promoted to captain and wrote a popular book, *The Voyage of Discovery*. By early 1907, he was already thinking about another Antarctic expedition.

THE RACE BEGINS

So far, neither the North or South Pole had been reached. At this point, Scott and Amundsen's attantions were focused on different poles: Amundsen on the North, and Scott on the South. That was about to change.

Meanwhile, on April 6, 1909, two Americans, Robert Peary and Matthew Henson, helped by a team of 24 Inuits and 130 dogs, claimed to have reached the North Pole.

At last! We've done it after 18 years and six attempts!

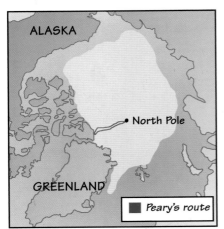

ALASKA

• North Pole

GREENLAND

■ Peary's route

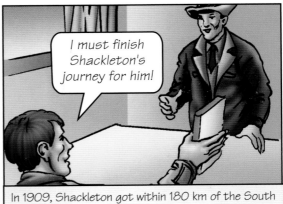

I must finish Shackleton's journey for him!

In 1909, Shackleton got within 180 km of the South Pole. Shackleton's success stung Scott into action.

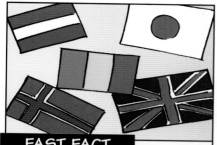

Amundsen had also been planning to reach the North Pole. He visited his hero, Nansen.

Can I borrow the Fram?

You'll have to persuade the government!

Amundsen got Fram and money from the government. Then, just before he was due to leave, the U.S. reached the North Pole.

I don't believe it! Peary got there first!

Now, I'll have to beat Scott to the South Pole!

By August 1910, Amundsen was ready to lead his own expedition to the South Pole, though the world thought he was headed to the North Pole.

I can't risk telling anyone—not even Nansen.

Scott was busy with his own preparations. Early in March 1910, he went to Norway to test the motor sledges for his expedition.

We will probably need to use animals as well.

Nansen introduced an expert skier, Tryggve Gran, to Scott.

Let me show you how easy it is on skis!

While in Norway, Scott also tried to meet Amundsen. But Amundsen wanted to keep his plans secret.

Can I speak to Mr. Amundsen?

Tell him I'm not here.

The Navy let Scott pick his own crew. Lieutenant Teddy Evans was put in charge of Scott's ship, the *Terra Nova*.

You'll have to work fast. We set sail in June.

Eight thousand men volunteered to go on the expedition. Scott chose 24.

Be warned. This is going to a be a long, hard journey.

The crew included several scientists, including experts in biology, geology, and meteorology.

There is so much we don't know about the Antarctic.

Captain Oates was put in charge of ponies bought in Siberia, Russia.

Scott also bought a few teams of sledge dogs, but after his bad experience with them on the *Discovery* expedition, he did not trust them.

Back in Norway, Amundsen studied Shackleton's 1909 expedition.

We only need a small team of skiers and dog sledges.

Amundsen ordered new skis, goggles, and sealskin clothes from Greenland.

These ski bindings are too tight.

Carpenter Jørgen Stubberud built a winter hut for the expedition in Amundsen's garden. It had 11 bunks and a separate room for cooking.

How quickly could you build it in the snow?

If we take the hut in sections, maybe just a couple of days.

Amundsen's men were all good skiers and used to the cold climate. Amundsen included a ski champion, Olav Bjaaland, in his team.

Bravo!

Amundsen believed the trek to the South Pole would be a long ski race. He took eight-foot skis made from solid wood to help his team cross deep crevasses.

The ski works like a bridge.

Amundsen did not want his men to pull sledges. It was too tiring. He took well-trained dogs, bought in Greenland, and two expert dog-handlers, Helmer Hanssen and Sverre Hassel.

Mush! Mush!

FAST FACT Huskies are part dog and part wolf. They will eat other dogs, so if a dog died, it could be fed to the rest of the team to keep them going.

JOURNEY TO THE SOUTH POLE

Scott and Amundsen were each determined to be the first to reach the South Pole. They left for Antarctica within days of each other. Amundsen was the first to set sail.

On June 7, 1910, the Fram left Christiania with 19 men, 97 dogs, a hut in sections, and provisions for two years. No one, besides Amundsen, knew they were heading for the South Pole.

We sail at midnight!

Aye, aye, Mr. Amundsen!

On June 15, 1910, the Terra Nova set sail. On board Scott's ship were 65 men, 3 motor sledges, 19 ponies, and 33 dogs. Thousands of people came to cheer them.

Hurray for Scott!

On September 6, the Fram docked at Madeira. Amundsen finally told his crew where they were going.

We're heading for the South Pole!

At first, Amundsen's crew were shocked. But they knew they were better skiers than Scott's party.

We'll race the English!

We'll get there first!

Amundsen sent a telegram to Scott, who had stopped off in Australia for supplies.

Amundsen's going for the South Pole, too!

If Amundsen wants a race, he's got one.

On November 29, 1910, the Terra Nova began the final leg of its voyage to the Antarctic. Three days later it was hit by a dangerous gale. The storm lasted 36 hours and nearly sank the ship.

Captain, two of the ponies have been killed!

Mr. Evans, we're taking on water fast! The pump is broken!

Arriving at Ross Island in January 1911, Scott found that ice blocked the way to the old hut from the *Discovery* expedition. He established a new base camp at Cape Evans, also on Ross Island.

Heave!

Within two weeks, a new hut was built and the supplies were brought ashore.

Mark each supply depot with a flag.

Whoa! Stop!

The depot teams were hit by blizzards. The ponies suffered very badly. On one occasion, the dogs pounced on a pony and attacked it.

Scott loved to watch the aurora, an amazing natural light show that occurs at both poles. Waves of green, purple, and blue light can fill the sky.

Finally, they set up the depots. Scott's team began their scientific studies. Herbert Ponting took photos of the local wildlife.

Once, Ponting was attacked by killer whales, but he managed to escape!

Help!

I'd better go out to check on the ponies.

On April 23, the sun sank below the horizon. It would not appear again until August. The long Antarctic winter had begun.

The hut was cramped, but there were happy moments. Scott celebrated his 43rd birthday.

Happy Birthday!

Amundsen reached Antarctica on January 14, 1911. He sailed to the Ross Ice Shelf and set up base camp in the Bay of Whales. His camp was 62 miles closer to the South Pole than Scott's, giving Amundsen a big advantage.

Look at those giant cliffs!

Bjaaland and Stubberud quickly put up the hut they had tested in Amundsen's garden. Named *Framheim* (home of Fram), this was their home for the long winter.

It's time to feed the dogs.

Hurry up, men! It will be dark soon.

Like Scott, Amundsen set up supply depots before starting the long journey to the South Pole, so they would not have to carry supplies for the entire journey.

We'll need this seal meat on on way back.

Setting up the depots meant traveling into unexplored territory in very bad weather. The dogs handled it very well.

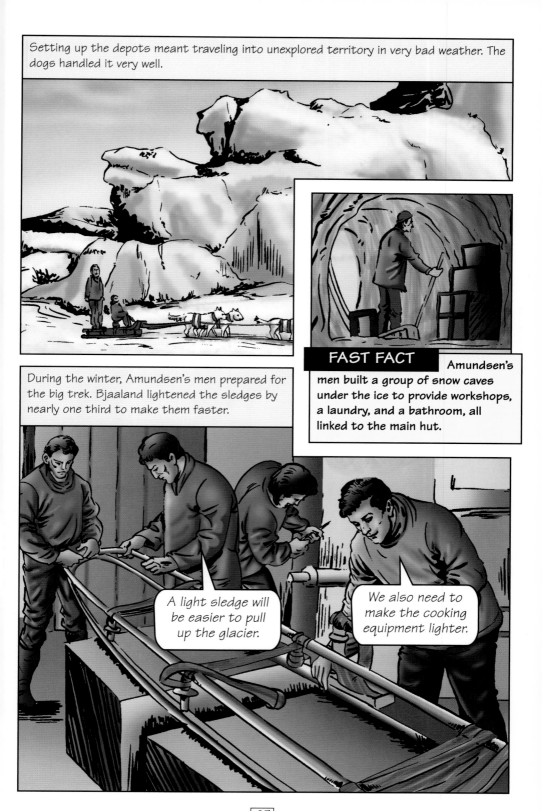

FAST FACT Amundsen's men built a group of snow caves under the ice to provide workshops, a laundry, and a bathroom, all linked to the main hut.

During the winter, Amundsen's men prepared for the big trek. Bjaaland lightened the sledges by nearly one third to make them faster.

A light sledge will be easier to pull up the glacier.

We also need to make the cooking equipment lighter.

AGAINST THE ELEMENTS

On October 20, 1911, Amundsen's team of five men, four sleds, and 52 dogs set off for the South Pole. They traveled the most direct route possible, going over, instead of around, anything that got in their way. They made good progress, traveling 20 miles each day.

On November 5, they reached their last supply depot. At this point, Amundsen's men were still 460 miles from the South Pole.

On November 11, Amundsen could see mountains in the distance. He named them *Queen Maud* after the Norwegian queen. His men began the long climb up the glacier, led by Bjaaland, the ski champion.

Luckily, the weather was good. By November 21, they had reached the summit. The dogs had pulled a ton of supplies to an altitude of 984 ft.

I'm sorry!

At the top, they shot 24 dogs to ration supplies. Eighteen dogs would be used in the final push to the South Pole.

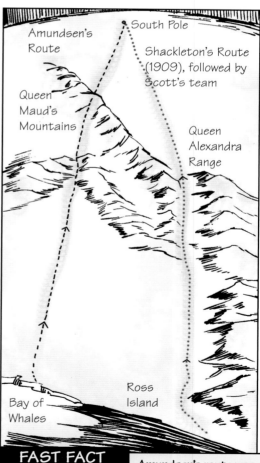

Amundsen's Route

South Pole

Shackleton's Route (1909), followed by Scott's team

Queen Maud's Mountains

Queen Alexandra Range

Ross Island

Bay of Whales

FAST FACT Amundsen's route was shorter, but he took a big risk. He could not be sure that there was a route over the mountains. Scott followed Shackleton's 1909 route.

Scott and his men began their trek to the South Pole on November 1, 1911. His party included two motor sledges and 10 men, each with a pony and sledge. Two others followed with dog sledges. The two motor sledges quickly broke down. Amundsen was already 200 miles ahead.

Pull!

It's no use. I can't get it started.

Soon, the ponies were in trouble, too.

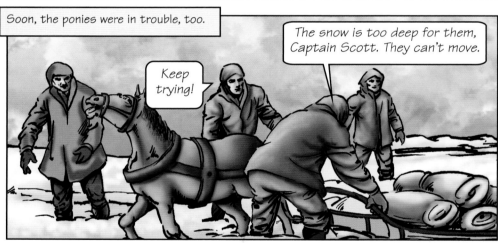

The snow is too deep for them, Captain Scott. They can't move.

Keep trying!

Every 70 miles, Scott's party set up new depots. Each contained enough food and fuel for a week for the return journey.

On December 5, a fierce blizzard hit Scott's men.

The wind is too strong.

We'll have to wait until the storm is over.

Cold hands and strong winds made it hard to put up tents.

The blizzard kept Scott pinned down for five days, wasting valuable time.

After the blizzard, the ponies could hardly stand. Since they could go no further, the last five ponies were shot for their meat.

FAST FACT

Harsh weather brought bad luck to Scott's team. The extreme cold killed many of his ponies.

From then on, Scott's men pulled their own sledges. The party of twelve, divided into groups, began to haul the sledges up the Beardmore Glacier toward the summit, 10,500 feet above.

Meanwhile, Amundsen's men were already at top, tackling the last difficult obstacle before reaching the South Pole. The Devil's Ballroom was a glacier with a thin crust of snow covering many dangerous, deep crevasses.

Whoa!
Slow down!

A few days away from the South Pole, Amundsen planted a black flag to let Scott know he was there already.

The real struggle for Scott's men had only just begun. Each man was pulling over 200 pounds, while sinking up to his knees in the snow.

Keep going, lads!

Blizzards made it impossible to see ahead.

Aaarrggghh!

Some of Scott's men suffered from snow blindness. Others fell into crevasses, pulling their sledges down with them. It was a hard trek. On December 13, Scott's men traveled just 4 miles in 9 hours.

We can't leave it behind, We need those supplies.

I can't see!

FAST FACT Snow blindness is a common problem for polar explorers. It is caused by bright sunlight reflecting off white snow and burning a person's eyes.

Meanwhile, helped by very good weather, Amundsen's team finally reached the South Pole on December 14, 1911. There was a loud cry of "Halt!" as the sledge meters showed they had arrived at the South Pole. The race to the South Pole had been won.

Amundsen's men set up camp. For three days, they made calculations to make sure that they really were at the South Pole.

There's no one else in sight!

They planted the Norwegian flag to show that they had reached the South Pole.

Admundsen and his team had a party in the tent that evening, and each man shared a little seal meat.

What a feast!

Amundsen put up a small tent with a message inside for Scott, along with a letter for Norwegian King Haakon.

Amundsen was excited to get back to base camp and spread the news. He did not know that Scott was almost 310 miles behind.

We need to tell the world that we got here first.

FAST FACT Trekking across the snow is hard work at high altitudes. Amundsen's men spent 16 hours a day in their sleeping bags, conserving their energy.

Down in the Beardmore Glacier, things were getting easier for Scott's men. They were starting to make good progress. The two remaining groups continued on.

On January 3, 1912, Scott chose four men to continue with him to the South Pole and told the other three to return. Lashly, Crean, and Evans were in tears as they turned back.

There was no sign of the Norwegians.

On January 13, Scott's team began the final leg to South Pole and in better spirits.

But it did not last long.

What's that over there?

They got here first!

On January 16, Scott's team came across Amundsen's flag and the remains of a camp along with tracks. Scott knew they had lost.

Scott felt responsible.

I've let everyone down.

FAST FACT During his travels, Scott wrote down his thoughts and feelings in notebooks. He was a very good writer, and his diaries remain an exciting read even today.

THE RACE ENDS

Scott reached the South Pole on January 17, 1912. He found Amundsen's tent and note—Amundsen had gotten there 33 days earlier. Scott planted the English flag, and Bowers took photos. But the men were in bad spirits, worn out by the long climb, only to find that they had lost the race to the South Pole.

Bowers
Captain Scott
Evans
Oates
Wilson

Meanwhile, Amundsen was one week from reaching base camp. His men were moving fast and in good spirits.

I'm starting to enjoy this!

Scott's party headed back. However, they were hit by blizzards again.

Things went from bad to worse for Scott's team. Evans got frostbite. Wilson was limping, and Scott hurt himself in a fall.

On February 7, they headed down the glacier. The men were getting weaker and weaker. Scott and Bowers discussed the shortage of food..

Why are we missing so much food?

Perhaps the returning party took too much by mistake.

Where is Evans?

He's dropped back. I think he's over there.

On February 11, Scott's team became lost for two days. He couldn't find the depot in the fog. They were now running out of food.

Evans was on his knees with a wild look in his eyes.

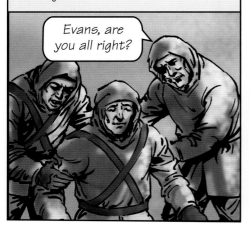

Evans, are you all right?

The men put Evans on a sledge and carried him to the next camp. He died at midnight.

Can't... go... on. . .

Amundsen and his crew arrived back at their base camp on January 25, 1912, 99 days and nearly 1,900 miles after their departure.

Look, they're back already!

Any chance of a cup of coffee?

Scott's men were in trouble. They were running out of the fuel they needed to make water from snow. There was a real danger of dying of thirst. Scott was also getting ill from a lack of vitamin C.

It's nearly all gone! This is getting worse and worse!

Temperatures were down to -40°F. The ground was so rough that even a strong wind in the sail would not budge the sledge.

How much longer can we keep this up?

At the next depot, the fuel had evaporated. The men were exhausted, frostbitten, and trapped by the storm. They knew they were doomed.

Oates could no longer hide his pain. His toes were black with frostbite. On March 16, Oates said he couldn't go on.

Don't give up. We'll get you back home.

The next morning, a blizzard howled outside...

"I am just going outside and may be some time."

Oates bravely stumbled out of the tent. The others knew he was walking to his death. Oates was never seen again.

The blizzard raged on for another ten days. Scott's last entry in his diary was on March 29, 1912. Half-starved and nearly frozen to death, Scott wrote 12 letters before he died.

"It seems a pity, but I do not think that I can write more. For God's sake, look after our people."

FAST FACT The memory of Scott's heroic failure lives on in his letters and his diaries, reprinted many times since his death.

They were just 11 miles from the next food depot. If only they had made it.

Eight months later, a search party found the frozen bodies of Scott, Bowers, and Wilson. Their tent was then collapsed over their bodies and a cairn was built to mark their grave. A pair of crossed skis was placed on top.

Poor men!

It took Amundsen a month to make the voyage back to Tasmania. Amundsen desperately wanted to be the first to announce his victory in the race to the South Pole.

On March 7, 1912, Amundsen finally telegraphed his brother, Leon, with the news, and it hit the newspapers.

What happened to Scott?

AMUNDSEN REACHES S. POLE

A year later, in February 1913, the *Terra Nova* reached New Zealand. The news of Scott's death caused a sensation in Britain.
A service was held in St. Paul's Cathedral to mark his death.

A memorial fund was used to pay off the expedition's debts, provide for the dead men's families, and set up the Scott Polar Research Institute, still in use today.

Roald Amundsen had many other polar adventures, including flying over the North Pole in a hot air balloon in 1926. But the poles would eventually claim his life, too. While on a rescue mission in 1928, Amundsen's plane crashed. He was never seen again.

When news of Scott's death was announced, people reacted more to Scott's tragic failure than to Amundsen's success. Amundsen's tactics of using skis and dogs were much better than Scott's motor sledges and ponies. Amundsen's only goal was to reach the South Pole first. Scott's goal, however, was to also carry out scientific studies while in Antarctica.

June 6, 1868: *Robert Falcon Scott born in Devon, England.*

June 16, 1872: *Roald Amundsen born at Borge near Christiania (Oslo).*

July 1881: *Scott joins Royal Navy.*

1888: *Nansen crosses Greenland from east to west.*

January 1898: *As part of* Belgica *expedition, Amundsen leads first skiing and sledging trips in Antarctica.*

Summer 1899: *Scott meets Clements Markham and applies to lead expedition.*

May 1900: *Scott is appointed leader of Antarctic expedition.*

January 1902: *Scott sights Antarctica.*

December 1902: *Scott, Shackleton, and Wilson get close to the South Pole.*

December 1906: *Amundsen's ship, the* Gjoa, *becomes first to navigate the Northwest Passage.*

January 9, 1909: *Shackleton's expedition turns back, just 112 miles from the South Pole.*

April 6, 1909: *Robert Peary claims to reach the North Pole.*

September 1909: *Scott announces second Antarctic expedition.*

September 9, 1910: *Amundsen sends telegram telling Scott he is heading for the South Pole.*

November 1910: Terra Nova *leaves New Zealand for Antarctica.*

January 4, 1911: Terra Nova *lands at Cape Evans.*

October 19, 1911: *Amundsen's party sets out for South Pole.*

November 1, 1911: *Scott's party sets out for the South Pole.*

December 14, 1911: *Amundsen's party reaches the South Pole.*

December 16, 1911: *Amundsen's party hoists the Norwegian flag at the South Pole.*

January 17, 1912: *Scott's party reaches the South Pole.*

February 17, 1912: *Evans dies.*

March 7, 1912: *Amundsen's* Fram *arrives in Tasmania to announce his victory.*

March 17, 1912: *Oates dies.*

March 29, 1912: *Probable date of death of Scott, Wilson, and Bowers.*

January 14, 1913: *Memorial service for Scott and his companions at St. Paul's Cathedral.*

November 6, 1913: *Scott's journals are published.*

June 18, 1928: *Amundsen dies somewhere in the Arctic in a plane crash.*

January 1957: *Amundsen-Scott South Pole station named after the two explorers.*

1. In an Antarctic blizzard, the wind creates a deafening roar. The fine snow stings the eyes and fills the nose and ears. People can get lost just a few steps from their shelter.

2. The Antarctic has most of the world's fresh water, but the water is frozen. Scott and Amundsen had to heat the ice to make water. When Scott ran out of fuel to melt the ice, he and his men were in danger of dying of thirst.

3. Husky dogs are built for living in the snow. Their thick hair keeps them warm. They just curl up tight and sleep in the snow.

4. The motor sledges that Scott brought to the Antarctic each cost the same as 660 husky dogs. They could only travel at 2–3 mph. They were heavy, too. One motor sledge broke through the ice as it was unloaded from the ship.

5. Antarctica is covered by an enormous sheet of ice. At its deepest point, it is 15,600 feet thick. It is formed by layers of snow falling year after year.

6. When the bodies of Scott and his party were found in 1912, 35 pounds of rocks were found by their tent. Among them were plant fossils showing the remains of lush forests covering the continent 250 million years ago.

7. Two rolls of film were also found in Scott's tent, frozen under the snow for eight months. Amazingly, the film survived and showed Scott and his team at the South Pole.

8. Because the wind is so strong in the Antarctic, explorers sewed their gloves onto cords attached to a harness over their jacket, so they would not lose them.

9. Both Scott and Amundsen depended on pemmican, dried meat mixed with fat. They also took biscuits that were so hard and were often soaked in hot cocoa to soften them.

10. Hoosh is the hot meal eaten on a sledging journey. It is a mix of pemmican, biscuit, and other ingredients, such as horse, seal meat, or chocolate.

11. Amundsen named one of the mountains in Antarctica after his housekeeper, Betty. She had knitted woolen vests for his whole team.

12. There is only one river in Antarctica, called the Onyx. It flows for just a few weeks each summer.

13. The first explorers used reindeer fur sleeping bags. The reindeer hairs stuck in their nose and mouth, and when the ice in their clothes melted, the bags became soggy and smelly.

GLOSSARY

Arctic: *The region around Earth's North Pole. The Arctic includes parts of Russia, Alaska, Canada, Greenland, Norway, as well as the Arctic Ocean. The boundary is usually considered to be the Arctic Circle, which is at the southern limit of the midnight sun.*

Antarctica: *The region around the South Pole. Unlike the Arctic, it is a solid continent and is almost entirely covered in ice. It is the coldest place on Earth.*

Blizzard: *A severe snowstorm caused by winds that move over 34 mph.*

Crampon: *A spiked, metal plate attached to the boot to help when walking on ice.*

Crevasse: *A deep crack in a glacier. Crevasses are often covered by snow and are difficult to see.*

Depot: *An area set up at various sites to provide supplies during an expedition.*

Evaporate: *When a liquid turns into a vapour and rises into the atmosphere.*

Expedition: *A journey undertaken by a group of people with a set objective, such as the exploration of new lands.*

Frostbite: *A condition, caused by extreme cold, that damages the skin and body tissues. Frost-bitten fingers and toes are white, cold, and numb. Gradually, they turn red and swollen, and finally tun black. If the tissue dies, the injured part must be cut off.*

Glacier: *A large river of ice that is formed on land and flows slowly downhill toward the sea.*

Hoosh: *The name for a hot meal eaten on a sledging journey, usually a porridge-like mixture of pemmican, biscuit, and other ingredients.*

Husky: *A breed of Arctic sled dog used by Amundsen and Peary. Many explorers bought dogs in Greenland and Russia and shipped them to the Antarctic.*

Ice: *Ice is frozen water. Most of the ice in Antarctica is made by falling snow that compresses over time, as it gets thicker and thicker.*

Ice floe: *Any piece of floating sea ice whose edges can be seen. It can be several miles across.*

Iceberg: *A massive floating island of ice that has broken away from a glacier or an ice shelf.*

Ice shelf: *A thick sheet of floating ice that forms on a polar coast. An ice shelf can extend hundreds of miles out to sea. Early explorers were awed by the white cliffs of the Ross Ice Shelf, called the* Barrier, *because it blocked the way to the South Pole.*

Inuits: *The native people of northern Arctic areas, once called* Eskimos.

Man-hauling: *People pulling sleds on foot, without the help of dogs or ponies. In deep snow, this can be incredibly exhausting.*

Magnetic poles: *Earth's magnetic field has two poles, one in the north and one in the south. Compass needles all point to the North Magnetic Pole.*

Midnight sun: *North of the Arctic Circle and south of the Antarctic Circle, the sun never sets in the summer months. It can be seen for 24 hours a day.*

Transantarctic Mountains: *The range of mountains that cross all of Antarctica and is one of the world's longest mountain chains. Amundsen and Scott each saw different parts of this range during their treks to the South Pole.*

Northwest Passage: *A sea route from the Atlantic to the Pacific through the Arctic Archipelago of northern Canada and along the northern coast of Alaska. Norwegian explorer Roald Amundsen led the first expedition across it between 1903–1906.*

Pack ice: *Pack ice is formed when the sea freezes. It may be a continuous sheet covering many square miles or be broken into many ice floes. These ice floes may be closely packed together or spread apart with channels of open water between them. The pressure from winds and currents can force pack ice to crush a ship.*

Pemmican: *A mix of dried beef, ground to a powder, and beef fat. Pemmican came from North American Indians, who pounded dried buffalo meat and mixed it to a paste with fat and berries.*

Scurvy: *A disease caused by deficiency of vitamin C, characterized by spongy and bleeding gums, bleeding under the skin, and extreme weakness.*

Sledge: *A wooden frame mounted on low runners that is pulled by working animals, such as horses or dogs. Sledges are used for transporting supplies across ice, snow, and rough ground.*

Snow blindness: *Damage to the eyes caused by the glare of reflected sunlight off snow. It is incredibly painful. Explorers affected by snow blindness bandaged their eyes and were tied to a sledge so they would not get lost.*

Tent: *A shelter, usually made of canvas or skins stretched over a frame of poles, that can be carried.. A special pyramid-shaped tent was used by Arctic explorers.*

Vitamin C: *A vitamin found naturally in plants, fruits, and vegetables that prevents or treats scurvy.*

Volcano: *An opening in Earth's crust from which molten lava, gas, and ash erupt onto the surface, sometimes forming mountains. In 1908, members of Shackleton's expedition were the first to climb Mount Erebus, Antarctica's most famous volcano.*

INDEX